THE **BRIDGE** TO **HOPE** & **HEALING**®

9 Principles to Guide You in a Moment of Crisis

Becky Schwartz Corbett
MSW, ACSW

BSCorbett Consulting, LLC
Rockville, Maryland

For information contact:
BSCorbett Consulting, LLC
info@bscorbettconsulting.com
http://www.bscorbettconsulting.com

Cover design by Mark David Robinson
Book design by Amy Forrester

ISBN-13: 978-0-9600511-9-9

L'Dor V'Dor
[from Generation to Generation]

To my namesakes:
my paternal and maternal great-grandmothers
Celia Sher Schwartz and Beck Kaufman Teller
may their memories forever be a blessing.
Although I never met you,
you provide me with wisdom and guidance.

CONTENTS

Introduction 1

Becky's Background 3

The Crisis 7

How to Use This Book 9

Hope...The fog will lift 13

Show strength and courage...Build your bridge 21

Maintain a positive outlook...Apply a strengths-based perspective 30

Communicate...Keep talking... 38

Seek resources...Invest in the relationships that sustain you 45

Heal...Take care of you.. 53

Accept, adjust, and affirm...Life moves forward 62

Forgive...Let go.. 69

Express gratitude...Count your blessings 75

Epilogue: From the other side of the bridge............................. 81

Acknowledgement 87

Notes 89

Becky's Bookshelf 91

Appendix.. 93

We live in a rainbow of chaos.
                              –Cezanne

INTRODUCTION

AS WE TRAVEL ALONG LIFE'S JOURNEY, we inevitably come face to face with hardship, disappointment, and crisis. Most people can get through the challenges, as it is human nature to survive. Yet, what if you could thrive? What if you could build a bridge and shape your path across a moment of crisis so that adversity does not negatively shape your life?

You cannot dictate when tragedy will strike, but you can control how you react to and handle it. I believe the choices we make and the actions we take in a moment of crisis clearly define who we are as individuals. When I faced a family crisis, it led to building my own bridge and realizing that I had an unique opportunity to share my story and inspire others.

My story is not one of betrayal. It is a story about a husband and wife who cared deeply for each other. It is about two people who threw out the divorce rule book, a wife who supported her husband through his coming-out process, parents who stayed focused on their daughter, and a family who built and crossed a bridge.

Building bridges is about creating connections, establishing relationships, and obtaining resources to help yourself. In a moment of crisis, we get thrown into a fog and often feel alone and confused, not knowing which way to turn. Yet you can learn how to build your bridge and create a vision, get through the fog, and cross to the other side.

The Bridge to Hope & Healing® is a guide featuring 9 Principles—techniques and concepts—to transform a moment of crisis by fostering a vision and moving it to action. The Principles will guide you toward the other side. Whether yours is a big or small crisis, these Principles are the place to start, providing models to follow, tips and techniques to revisit, and journal reflections and prompts to facilitate building your own bridge. A crisis will eventually fade. However, the healing journey is a personal process that takes time and is also a choice. *The Bridge to Hope & Healing*® is a decision to stand firm on the other side and look back at how far you have come.

BECKY'S BACKGROUND

I WAS BORN CELIA REBECCA SCHWARTZ—always going by Becky—into a southern Jewish family in New Orleans, Louisiana. I grew up with six (three sets of) grandparents and received my Master of Social Work from The University of Alabama. These are the three aspects of my personal history I identify as having the biggest impact on my journey to build *The Bridge to Hope & Healing*®.

Southern Jewish Roots. My upbringing in Judaism could not be characterized as religious or even particularly observant. As with all of my peers in our southern Jewish community, I went to religious school once a week and Temple for services for the High Holy days. This is where I was taught about Judaism. It was, however, through participation in Jewish youth group activities and attending Henry S. Jacobs Camp[1] every summer that I learned how to *be* Jewish. These community activities nurtured the growth of my intrinsic spirituality, giving me a sense of belonging, a connection to others, and a place of peace. Over time, this matured into my Jewish identity, my belief system, and my ability to hope.

Throughout my story, I incorporated Hebrew words and phrases that have brought me comfort and strength. English translations bracketed next to each Hebrew transliteration will help readers to understand these terms in context.

Core Value. Family is important. Today, divorce and step-families are common. Yet when my father's parents divorced in 1946, they had no idea that the foundation of family they would create would one day have its own vocabulary. I grew up in a blended family. Both of my paternal grandparents re-married when my father was still young. When I later arrived, the granddaughter of six grandparents, I never heard the term *step* (as in step-parent), and *in-laws* was just a label. Everyone was family.

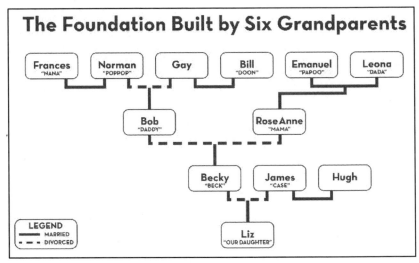

This is not a comprehensive representation of Becky's family tree.

This sense of family can be attributed to my Nana (Frances Wallach Weissberger Schwartz), who joined the *mishpachah* [family] in 1948 when she married her second husband, PopPop (my paternal grandfather, Norman Schwartz). From the beginning, Nana was a model for the family, demonstrating the acceptance and friendship that defines us today. She simply lived her philosophy: *It's family*. From this I learned, absorbed, and created my philosophy: W*e do not give away family members, we just keep adding and adding and adding family to our lives.*

Nana (fondly nick-named Nana Banana) lived to be 103 and a half years old and, throughout my life, was a source of personal strength and the foundation from which I developed the Principles for building *The Bridge to Hope & Healing*®. Her guidance, mentorship, and support always provided hope and a positive outlook through my own moments of crisis and hardship.

From Multiple Family Crises to Social Work. I first faced family crisis when I was 18. While at college, I received a call that my grandfather Doon had shot my paternal grandmother Gay and then turned the gun on himself. In 1988, the phrase *elderly suicide* had not yet been coined. You can imagine the confusion and pain of dealing not only with the loss of my grandparents, but with a subject concealed by society. My initial memory of receiving this horrific news is the support and care provided by my University of Alabama classmates and Sigma Delta Tau[2] sorority sisters, as well as childhood friends from camp and middle-school. It was their warmth and love that I most clearly remember. My friends may not be able to recall this moment, but I do. We were just kids and no one really knew what to do or say, yet they were present with hugs, to coordinate my trip home to New Orleans, and to sit beside me.

My next significant memory of this crisis was at home. Of course, Nana was at the funeral, along with Dada and Papoo (my maternal grandparents, Leona and Emanuel Teller). Present and nurturing, together my grandparents took care of me. And that night, it was Nana's son from her first marriage, Uncle Larry, who stayed up all night with me. He provided generous support and love and used his own clinical social work training to help me be strong for my parents and to acknowledge my own anger and frustration.

Three years later, right after mailing the invitations to my wedding, I learned that my father had asked my mother for a divorce. The splitting of one's parents is an upheaval at any age, and this timing amplified the tension. I think about receiving comfort from family and friends, most specifically, Nana reminding all of us that we remain a family and that divorce does not change the fact that you still have a mom and a dad.

I did survive these events, but not without these situations for-ever shaping my life. Most visibly, they would be a major influence toward my shifting to a helping profession in college. I first changed my major from business to human development and family studies, then earned a graduate degree in social work. In the long run, these life-changing moments would guide the social worker I became, my resilience to life, and my own response to crisis.

THE CRISIS

ALL OF MY LIFE'S EXPERIENCES prepared me for the morning I gave James Casey Corbett (Case), my husband of 15 years, the most beautiful five-page letter[3] I had ever written—and likely will ever write. That evening, we faced what I had suspected: he is gay. At that moment, on that day, my life changed forever. As they say, "Life isn't measured by the number of breaths we take, but by the moments that take our breath away."

My world came crashing down on that crisp fall day. My husband was my best friend. That night, we held each other, we cried, and we talked for hours. I felt as if I were in a fog, unable to see clearly. Yet, despite my inability to truly comprehend what was happening, I had the intuition to start asking myself questions: "Why can't I keep my dear friend of almost 20 years, my soon-to-be former husband, in my life? Why can't I have a divorce that matters? Why can't I have a divorce that people actually envy? Why does a family have to only be defined as a husband, wife, and child? Why can't we *still* be a family?"

It wasn't long before my brain started to overflow with an abundance of positive thoughts and I began creating my vision of a *new* Corbett family. I said to Case, "I don't know how we will get from point A to point B, but we will. After all, *we are* a family." I really had no idea at that moment how and what we would even tell our daughter Liz, who was in fifth grade. However, what I instantly knew deep inside was that we needed support. The very first resource that came to mind was an individual from our own religious community—after all, he is gay, too. I told my husband he had 48 hours to call Cantor Larry Eschler—he would know what to do. And Case did.

I thought about Nana living her life with three families, and I made the decision that, with passion and compassion, Case, Liz, and I could thrive. Building upon my Judaism, social work knowledge, and relationships with family and friends, I set out on a journey to live my core value—*family is important.* I chose to embrace what Nana modeled to shape my actions and build our own bridge across this crisis.

The pain and struggles that followed were very real. It wasn't a simple process and it took time. The bridge we built did not happen overnight. It often required going back to Nana to keep us on track. Upon reflection, I clearly see how these Principles could help guide me through any crisis. Looking back on this experience, I saw the bridge that had emerged. Upon completing the first draft of this manuscript, I realized that this is the book I wish I had.

HOW TO USE THIS BOOK

MY PURPOSE IN WRITING THIS BOOK is to give you the gift that Nana gave me—hope, a positive outlook, and Principles to incorporate into your life so that you can live in the beauty of your own rainbow and with a sense of internal *Shalom* [peace]. Whether dealing with a health issue, struggling with addiction, the loss of a job, suicide of a loved one, a natural disaster, or the death of a family member, the Principles are a guide to assist you through your crisis and beyond. By sharing my story, I illustrate the power of hope and healing while explaining concepts, information for integrating the Principles into your life, and practical techniques.

Building a bridge to hope and healing includes Principles that are part of a continuum. Although numbered one to nine, they are not meant to be sequential steps. To support you through the process, each Principle culminates with three strategies: Tips & Techniques, a Bridge Reflection, and Journal Prompts. These provide immediate solutions that can be integrated into your hope and healing journey. Throughout my multiple crises, I tried all of these strategies, learning what works best in what circumstance. Over time, I began to rely on those healthy behaviors and practices that best nurtured my well-being.

Tips & Techniques provide examples of a variety of these practices, underscoring that healing is a process and comes from within. It requires attention to the mind, body, and spirit. As such, a healing journey is also an opportunity to both recover from a crisis *and* intentionally grow in other areas of your life. Bridge

Reflections offer inspiration for you to reflect, be present, and focus on building your bridge. The Journal Prompts help navigate your own journey and guide you in applying the concepts to your unique circumstance.

Journal writing allows you to express yourself in a confidential manner, releasing tension, anger, frustrations, and disappointments. It gives you a means to think through your thoughts, feelings, and beliefs, as well as the ability to look back and read about where you were physically, emotionally, and intellectually during a particular moment. Take the time to secure a quiet space, read the reflection, pause, and complete the Journal Prompts. This is a good place to start.

This book is for you to use in a moment of crisis. It will necessitate strength and courage to begin. In each life circumstance, your role is to identify the concepts that resonate with your core values, reflect on them, and implement the ones that encourage you to build *your* bridge to hope and healing. Use the Principles freely and flexibly to guide you and employ the Tips & Techniques, Bridge Reflections, and Journal Prompts to assist along your growth journey. The approach is adaptable to individual needs and dispositions and will further stimulate ideas for creating your own strategies.

JOURNAL PROMPTS

To begin building your bridge to hope and healing, start with these journal prompts.

My moment of crisis is...

_____

_____

_____

_____

_____

_____

_____

My core values are...

_____

_____

_____

_____

_____

_____

_____

_____

_____

_____

_____

I want to survive and thrive through this life
circumstance because...

My vision for building my bridge to
hope and healing is...

PRINCIPLE #1

Hope...The fog will lift

Hope is a way of thinking, feeling, and acting. It is necessary for when a life-changing moment of crisis suddenly throws you in a fog, leaving you with a flood of emotions—feeling lost, confused, overwhelmed, or helpless.

Tomorrow is another day.
—Nana

M Y HUSBAND CAME OUT AND THE FOG SET IN. When I face a major upheaval, it is like a foggy lens is over my eyes. Crisis provokes shock and dismay so that I cannot even see clearly. Soon after my husband acknowledged that he is gay, my sight was literally blurred, yet my ophthalmologist insisted that I was fine and had 20/20 vision.

This fog also distorted my faculties. One day, I couldn't find my checkbook (yes, this was 2006, and we still used paper checks). I had just written a check the day before and was sure I had returned the checkbook to its proper file drawer. A few days later, I went to the extra freezer in the storage room to get some pot roast out for dinner. When I opened the door, staring back at me was the checkbook. Funny now, but quite disconcerting at the time.

A few weeks later at work, my boss asked for a specific report of which I had absolutely no recollection. This was an unusual occurrence for me. I was the Director of Administration for a non-profit organization and routinely managed multiple people and projects with high confidence and competence. Although I was able to produce the report in time for our meeting, my head was swimming. "Where did that report come from? How did it appear in my files? Who wrote it? ME? How did I write it? When did I write it?"

While in the fog, you may go through life barely remembering what you did.

A key concept toward building a bridge out of the fog is, simply, hope. You have to begin with a little belief and trust that it will be okay...even if you aren't sure. Hope does have a universal purpose, although the source for hope is unique to each individual. It is a psychological asset to guard against despair, provide a coping mechanism, and enhance quality of life. Hoping is not wishing; it is a way to think, feel, and act.[4] As my dear friend and colleague Betsy Clark recently wrote, *Choose Hope* (*always choose hope*).[5]

During foggy moments, it's okay to simply go through the motions of living. You stick to your calendar even though you may not want to. Through routine, you restore your equilibrium, and eventually your zeal.

The evening after the initial conversation with Case, we hosted our annual Halloween party. Only one couple knew we were experiencing a family crisis. The party had already been scheduled and cancelling would not have changed the situation. Sometimes the best thing to do is keep moving forward.

The fog will take time to lift, and each step you take moves you further along. For two weeks following Halloween, I didn't talk to anyone about our situation. When I woke up the next Saturday morning, I was ready to break my silence. It was time to take some kind of action. I called Nana and Uncle Larry, the family members who I knew—without hesitation—would be supportive of my family. Friends and family can give you hope that it will be okay, and they can help guide you through the fog.

A week later, I was on the train to spend the weekend with Nana. Alone in my thoughts, I didn't know what to do. I had the book *The Other Side of the Closet*[6] clutched by my side, though I couldn't focus and read quite yet. I started to type in my journal and surprisingly found comfort in words popping up on the screen. I typed thoughts, feelings, ideas, encouragement, frustration, anger, riddles, and poems. Journaling has proven physical and mental health benefits, and in this moment—I was just trying to establish order in a world that had been thrown into chaos. Talking (and listening) to myself through writing eased my way through the fog and would become a valuable tool throughout my healing journey.

Shortly after speaking with Case, Cantor Larry Eschler reached out to check on me. Simply receiving a call from someone brought me hope. He was so calm, so kind, so thoughtful, and this began a new connection that would continue beyond the crisis. From this experience, Cantor Larry would become my spiritual advisor. I would understand that my Judaism is the foundation for my hope, and I would learn to rely on my spirituality for healing.

In times of distress, it is common to be oblivious to others around you who are helping, or to even fight those trying. Metaphorically, if a thick fog sets in over your bridge, you may not even know the bridge is there. While in the fog, I met with a colleague and friend who instantly knew something was wrong. I was totally unaware that I had lost 20 pounds in 20 days. She had me sit on her couch and directed me to eat a burger, and I did. I had no appetite, but I consumed the burger because she told me to. The nourishing food and company moved me one step further toward healing. Obstinacy will not undo the crisis and allowing others to help can give you much needed support along your journey.

It is essential to understand that the fog will lift. You breathe and take it one day at a time, perhaps one hour at a time, or even one moment at a time, and, occasionally, one minute at a time. In my family, when any difficulty happened, we were taught to breathe, particularly during the initial moment that throws you into the fog. You take a deep breath in, slowly breathe out, and repeat. I have since learned that there are actual physical and psychological benefits to regulating your breathing. When you emerge from the initial fog, you begin to see clearly and find yourself on the bridge. Hazy moments will reappear, though now you recognize hope and trust that you will get through the fog.

> *We must accept finite disappointment,*
> *but never lose infinite hope.*
> −Dr. Martin Luther King, Jr.

TIPS & TECHNIQUES

---

* ❖ When you experience a foggy moment, recognize you are having an incident. Stop doing what you are doing. Take a deep breath. *Breathe*. Remind yourself, "the fog will lift." Sometimes you feel as if you can't breathe, but you do, and you can. *Breathe*. *Breathe* again. Take one breath at a time and keep breathing.

* ❖ Breathing meditation exercise to restore inner peace:
    Step 1: Sit up straight and relax your arms
    Step 2: Close your eyes
    Step 3: Take a deep breath—inhaling through your nose
    Step 4: Hold your breath for 3 seconds
    Step 5: Open your mouth—exhaling slowly, push all the air from your chest
    Step 6: Repeat steps 3 through 5, at least 9 more times

❖ Time is your new favorite four-letter word. Give the fog time to lift and give yourself time to heal. Healing is a journey and some moments of crisis take longer to recover from than others. Everyone's journey is different.

❖ During foggy moments, it's okay to just go through the motions of living. External practice eventually becomes a natural routine. Visualize yourself walking through the fog and over the bridge. Let your friends and family help guide you. Things will become clearer and you *will* feel like yourself once again.

❖ Be kind and gentle to yourself. You have to take care of YOU before you can take care of anyone else. If you aren't going to, who is? Ask yourself, "What may give me a sense of peace, calm, serenity?" Give a little gift to yourself every day. Buy a piece of your favorite candy or flowers, take a bubble bath, or read inspirational quotes.

❖ Once you emerge from the initial daze, foggy moments will reappear. Years later, a place or a certain date may trigger a memory and the fog will come back. However, it is less dense each time. If you find yourself back on the bridge, keep walking; this time it won't be as long. Have a little hope. The fog *will* lift.

BRIDGE REFLECTION

A Letter to God from the Fog
by Becky S. Corbett

Dear God, please lift the fog—I need a little hope to see again. I do want to move forward and I need the strength and courage to create a new definition of family.

Please God, lift the fog—I need a little inspiration to keep me out of the darkness so that I can affirm my love for life. I need the strength and courage to release the harmful emotions and unleash the ability to take care of ME.

Please God, lift the fog—I need the strength and courage to focus on the relationships that sustain me and tell the people I love how much they mean to me.

Please God, lift the fog so that I can live in peace once again.

And, God, one more thing, please give me the strength to do the best I can. I have been given an opportunity to truly discover myself, to look deep within and become me. It takes strength and courage to do this. Often, it seems unbearable. Let me choose my path with integrity because at the end of the day, I have to live with ME.

Todah Rabah [Thank you very much].
Rivka [Rebecca]

Rivka means Rebecca and is the Hebrew name given to Becky as an infant during the ceremony to welcome her into the covenant of the Jewish people.

JOURNAL PROMPTS

The fog feels like...

_____
_____
_____
_____
_____
_____
_____
_____
_____
_____

Hope means...

_____
_____
_____
_____
_____
_____
_____
_____
_____
_____
_____
_____

Today is a difficult day to cut through the fog, so I will...

_____

_____

_____

_____

_____

_____

_____

_____

_____

I bring hope into my life when...

_____

_____

_____

_____

_____

_____

_____

_____

_____

_____

PRINCIPLE #2

Show strength and courage...
Build your bridge

Show strength and courage by living your core values—it gives you the capacity to build your bridge to hope and healing.

> *Family is everything.*
> *—Nana*

MY HUSBAND IS GAY—NOW WHAT? I remember praying to God to give me the strength to ask for help and the courage to stay a family. In times of crisis, professionals talk of resiliency or simply being able to effectively deal with adversity and handle change. Likewise, your level of resilience is how well you will respond to a crisis. And there is little doubt that overcoming a life-changing moment requires incredible strength and courage. You need courage to define your bridge and the inner strength to move to action.

My vision was keeping my family together. I wanted to take the best of the *old* Corbett family and transform it into the *new* Corbett family. Doing so would include establishing a renewed relationship with my husband, as well as accepting a wider definition of family. As with maintaining hope, building this bridge starts with trust—

trust in yourself and in your instincts. Although everyone around me was saying, "You are so strong and courageous," my world was crashing inside. While it seemed too painful to go on, it was critical to keep facing my fear of losing my family and reach for sources of strength and courage. Cultivating resources actually improved my resiliency. So, even when I didn't believe I could do it, I trusted my intuition and kept repeating to myself, "You have the strength and courage to keep your family together."

In the short term, merely telling oneself to be brave and strong can be profoundly beneficial in navigating difficult times. It is a simple and effective strategy to develop belief in your ability to face coming challenges. At first, I just *acted* with fortitude. In time, I gained internal strength and courage in my actions to establish my vision for thriving through this crisis, and I developed the *chutzpah* [the audacity] to redefine my family.

Strength and courage can be attained from the support of others. My former husband and I maintained a level of trust and partnership that, although unusual in divorce, was critical in building our bridge. Through all the heartache, I never believed he had set out to purposely betray himself, me, or our daughter. I felt baffled, but not tricked or deceived. Dealing with this confusion was a significant component of my healing journey. The trust we had for one another was enough to give me the courage to rely on our common values to make the commitment to *be* a family. We threw out the rule book and set out on a journey together to ignore societal pressures, create our own path, and redefine family.

To build a bridge, it is necessary to find the strength and courage to educate oneself. To guide our family's path, I wanted and needed to comprehend what my husband was going through. I talked with gay friends and read books. I went to a Lambda Legal[7] function in Chicago with a childhood friend who came out on his 30th birthday. I donated to the Human Rights Campaign.[8] I discussed the coming-out process with my mental health therapist. I reached out to a family friend whose husband came out in the 1970s, and to friends with gay children. I even attended a dinner party hosted by my gay cousins and observed as they celebrated my husband's coming out.

I gained additional strength and courage to educate myself by focusing on our daughter Liz. At 10 years old, she had her own unique journey and now had to process what I refer to as "divorce squared"—her parents' divorce along with having a gay father. Learning about the coming-out process helped me be a more informed parent, gave me the language to talk with my daughter, and allowed me to be a role model for our community.

Concentrating on our daughter ensured we would maintain family time and holiday traditions, although a new version. When Case moved to his apartment, Liz and I assisted. We continued to have family dinners. The Jewish holiday of Passover[9] is a cornerstone to our family that pre-dates our daughter, and we continued to celebrate together. Preserving the tradition of hosting the Passover Seder[10] for our extended family kept me centered.

Having the strength and courage to live your vision often generates additional struggle. Although we were determined to surround ourselves with individuals and communities who embraced the *new* Corbett family, even with the best plan, not everyone close to us understood. There were some people who choose not to support you, perhaps because of their own insecurities, religious beliefs, unresolved issues, or capacity. When someone is presented an unfamiliar, or perhaps taboo situation, you may be holding up a mirror to them. In other words, if you stand close enough to another person and look into each other's eyes, you actually see your own reflection, not the other individual. As a dear friend explained to me, by revealing the truth you may scare people. You need to realize that negative reactions may reflect others' lives and not actually be pointed at you.

As I began telling my story, I was able to gauge others by their facial expressions. I also discovered through spiritual guidance with Cantor Larry that *people will react to how you react*. If I expressed anger and resentment toward Case, others would, too. So I mustered the strength and courage to literally stare at myself in the mirror and envision what I wanted to see. I visualized myself walking across the bridge as a caped *Superwoman*, standing proudly alongside *my* family, with our daughter seeing a mom and dad united and who respected and cared deeply for one another.

It was quite daunting to risk my secure life and find the courage to write and the strength to actually give my husband the letter[3] that opened our dialog. The alternative of not feeling at peace in our marriage and continuing to live my life with something missing was shattering me inside. I repeatedly reminded myself that I could choose to change from this crisis. I often relied on my *Superwoman* image and held onto my belief that every life experience shapes us into the person we are to become. I had been given a gift—to take a family crisis, which created a loss—and although it scared me, I embraced my inner superpower to grow and develop personally.

> *Do not go where the path may lead.*
> *Go instead where there is no path and leave a trail.*
> −Ralph Waldo Emerson

TIPS & TECHNIQUES

- ❖ Before moving to action, take a deep breath. *Breathe.* Say to yourself, "I have the strength and courage to trust myself and build my bridge to hope and healing." *Breathe.*

- ❖ Move one healing technique to action today. Begin anywhere. Just begin. Do one thing. It doesn't matter what. Take a leap of faith, jump, and go for it.

- ❖ Don't give up on your dreams—in fact, *chase* your dreams. Dream big, then dream even bigger. Grow those thoughts into a vision that aligns with your core values, live those values, and *be* your bridge.

- ❖ Mirror reflection exercise to live with integrity:
    Step 1: Take a deep breath and breathe
    Step 2: Look into the mirror and see your true reflection
    Step 3: Evaluate your thoughts, feelings, and actions
    Step 4: Reflect upon what you have learned from this crisis
    Step 5: Ask yourself, "Who do I want to be in this set of circumstances?"

- ❖ Give yourself the gift of self-awareness throughout your healing journey. Choose to turn a difficult situation into a personal growth opportunity. Strive to learn and improve as an individual.

- ❖ Write in a journal. Spill out your emotions, thoughts, feelings—anything that comes to mind. Choose a time that is best for you and find a quiet place. Sit down, alone in your thoughts, and write without passing judgment. Write on paper—seeing your comments in your own handwriting makes your situation real. Review your journal entries. Go back and read about what you were thinking and feeling at a particular moment. Reflect on how far you have come and where you still want to grow.

❖ Do your homework and educate yourself about this life circumstance in order to best understand and make informed decisions. Use the Internet for reputable online resources, such as websites, books, organizations, blogs, and videos. Explore all medications and treatment options for medical conditions. Obtain referrals for attorneys and mediators for legal issues. Be analytical, seek data and statistics, and learn pricing options.

❖ Create an action plan which provides a framework to keep moving forward along your hope and healing journey. Stay focused on yourself and identify important milestones. Push yourself to establish realistic goals that will help you through each moment.

BRIDGE REFLECTION

On Becoming
by Cantor Larry Eschler

Sometimes, along life's journey, we all need to be reminded that we have the power to *become*.

The true difficulty in becoming is—we are impatient. Becoming is a process.

Learning a new skill, having a relationship or leaving a relationship, growing up or growing old, and even having an illness or healing is a becoming. As adults, we may forget that all different becomings take time and effort, and that to *become*, we must give ourselves the space and time for these changes.

We must realize that what is important is to have enough consciousness to choose the becoming or, in the case of something that happens to us, to choose who we will be in that set of circumstances.

We really have two choices: we can choose to become what we want, or we can be molded by outside forces such as the people around us or the situation we find ourselves in—becoming what we feel someone else wants us to be.

Eschler, L. (2014). *Temple Beth Ami Chadashot*. 43(4) 1/18. Rockville, MD: Temple Beth Ami. (*reproduced with permission*)

JOURNAL PROMPTS

I obtain strength and courage from...

....

....

....

....

....

....

....

I will trust myself to...

....

....

....

....

....

....

....

....

....

....

....

Regardless of distraction, I will stay focused on my
vision and be true to my core values because...

_____

_____

_____

_____

_____

_____

_____

I can and will build my bridge to
hope and healing because...

_____

_____

_____

_____

_____

_____

_____

_____

_____

_____

_____

PRINCIPLE #3

Maintain a positive outlook... Apply a strengths-based perspective

---

A positive outlook is focusing on strengths and believing your life is overflowing—not living your life as half-empty or half-full.

> *Choose to be positive.*
> —Nana

I DID NOT CHOOSE FOR MY HUSBAND TO BE GAY, and the thought of divorce distressed me. I had every right to be in a fog, to be outraged by Case, to blame the gay community, to be frustrated by people around me, and to wallow in my own self-pity. After all, it is natural to be consumed by negativity in a crisis.

During a disruptive or life-changing event, it is nearly impossible to avoid adverse emotional and psychological states of mind—anger, anxiety, depression. Everyone's individual response to a crisis is unique, and it is common to not focus on the positive. Yet, in every circumstance, there is always choice, and in any crisis there comes a time to take action, to build and walk across your bridge. You can either choose to let the negative feed, grow stronger, and paralyze you, or you can choose to learn, gaining a wider perspective.

Professionals refer to this as positive reframing. Many studies illustrate how positive or negative thinking affects our mental health and our individual resilience—how we cope with a crisis. Although reframing difficulties and trying to find something good in them is simple in theory, it is rarely easy in practice. Choosing to see the glass half full, or even overflowing, will not, by itself, resolve the situation. Still, maintaining a positive outlook illumi-nates solutions and keeps you from wallowing in the negative. A strengths-based perspective can be a valuable response to crisis.

In full transparency, I have a hard time being negative. Even in the worst of situations, those moments are brief. I typically look at a dark cloud and identify the silver lining. For example, I was getting a divorce, however my daughter still had a father; and even though my husband is gay, we could remain a family and stay friends. Negative thinking emanates from strong emotions and reframing is effective. Although a conventional expression, I was troubled when I realized that after our divorce, I would be referred to as an *ex-wife*. I truly didn't see myself as "out of" a relationship with Case. So instead, I redefined the characterization. I held my head high and proudly owned the label as I started referring to myself as a *former wife*. Taking my cue, and also choosing to have a positive outlook, Case started introducing me as his *only wife*. While funny, it also made me feel good and led me to redefine my situation as the former wife of an amazing gay man, dedicated father, and dear friend.

Positive reframing is a practice that can be learned and provides definite benefits. A few months later, I mustered enough strength and courage to walk into a setting that I was forewarned could be highly charged. It was a support group in which I actually did find 80 percent of the room angry and stuck. My initial reaction was that *everyone* was negative, and I needed to run far away. Yet these were my sisters and brothers by circumstance—their spouses were gay, too—and so I stayed. Drawing on my optimism and my social work training, I was able to find strength in the situation, as well as from their affirming stories. I chose to focus on the 20 percent of individuals that were creating their own positive healing journey, just like me. I realized I wasn't alone and that my new friends would *always* understand *my* side of the closet. I remained hopeful that the others would find the constructive aspects of their situations and understand they have the potential to do much more—together we would heal and grow.

You know your thoughts,
but everyone sees only your attitude.
—H. Jackson Brown, Jr.

TIPS & TECHNIQUES

* ❖ When you want to be positive, choose to see the glass as overflowing. Take a deep breath. *Breathe.*

* ❖ Identify the quality of life you desire and live your life the way you want. Do not let your current situation define you. Redefine and revitalize your situation by reframing negative thoughts and feelings.

* ❖ Consistently give yourself positive affirmations. Hold your head up high, look at yourself in the mirror, and be proud of who you are. Talk positively to you about YOU. We would never tolerate someone speaking negatively to our children or loved ones the way we sometimes speak to ourselves. Choose to focus on individual strengths.

* ❖ People will react to how you react. If you express resentment, so will others. When you feel angry, upset, annoyed, frustrated, or jealous, recognize the emotion, acknowledge it, accept it, and find a healthy release. When you treat others with respect and kindness, others will treat you respectfully, too. Model the behavior you want to see in others. Your actions speak louder than words. Focus on children, whether your nieces, nephews, friends', your own, or your grandchildren. Ask yourself, "If a child were standing beside me, is this what I would say or do?"

* ❖ Read, collect, and use positive and motivational quotes to give you daily inspiration. Find quotes on websites or apps, imprinted on signs, or from spiritual and religious sources. Write the quotes that speak to you on post-it notes. Rotate and strategically place them where they are easily visible, such as next to your bed, on the bathroom mirror, or in your office.

❖ Use humor. Sometimes in difficult situations, all we can do is laugh. Laughter releases tension and humor goes a long way. Laugh out loud, laugh hard, and laugh often. Belly laugh so hard that you cry.

❖ Make a victory list at the end of each day and include the small tasks you completed as well as the big accomplishments. Give yourself a pat on the back, smile, and let go of everything you didn't get done. Initially, as you experience a moment of crisis, it will be sufficient just to get out of bed and get dressed. As time progresses, your victory list will multiply.

❖ Choose happiness and go have some fun. Do something, anything that makes you smile. Watch a sitcom, go to a comedy club, plan a day trip to an amusement park, hang out with a 2-year-old—there is nothing like the sound of a child's giggle lingering in the air. As we say in New Orleans, *laissez les bons temps rouler* [let the good times roll].

BRIDGE REFLECTION

The Energy Dance: A Poem of Enlightenment
by Becky S. Corbett, aka, The Blossoming Healer

To experience DahnMuDo, an energy dance, is to be awakened.

To experience DahnMuDo enlightens.

To experience an energy dance is to be at peace with oneself.

To experience DahnMuDo helps one to realize you have been given another chance to create your life the way it was always meant to be created.

To experience an energy dance gives you the space to fully accept who you are.

After experiencing DahnMuDo, an energy dance, my promise to my enlightened soul...
  I will accept when things happen.
  I will stay calm.
  And when I feel a negative emotion, I will embrace the feeling and then "let it go."
  I will remind myself daily that I am courageous, precious, and beautiful.
  And when I get lost, I will bring myself back to DahnMuDo, so that I can create, again.

Poem written by Becky after receiving the name *Blossoming Healer* during Dahn Yoga's Shim Sung Heart Chakra Workshop, June 8, 2018. Becky participated in DahnMuDo, an energy dance in a meditative state where you feel free in your mind and body as you naturally flow with the energy (www.bodynbrain.com/body-brain-yoga).

JOURNAL PROMPTS

When someone is negative, it makes me feel/want to...

I take a difficult situation and turn it into something positive by...

When I am disappointed by someone, I will identify the individual's strength by...

_____

_____

_____

_____

_____

_____

_____

_____

Something positive that can come from this difficult situation is...

_____

_____

_____

_____

_____

_____

_____

_____

_____

PRINCIPLE #4

Communicate...Keep talking

Communication happens when two people continue to talk, truly listen, and express what they intend.

> *Keep talking.*
> —Nana

TWO WEEKS AFTER MY HUSBAND CONFIRMED what I had suspected—he is gay—I took the train to New York to talk with Nana and Uncle Larry. I intuitively knew they would be able to advise me. As I had been feeling lonely in my own home for so long, Nana's house was the ultimate place of comfort. It provided me with much needed *Shalom bayit* [peace of the home], a safe space, a home to gather love and support.

Upon my arrival, I had barely let go of Nana's warm hug when she whisked me off for a slice of New York pizza. No talking; she was nourishing my body and soothing my soul. Back at her house, she made me her signature drink, an Old Fashioned. She reminded me that in times of trouble and celebration, our family has *one* drink and emphasized "everything in moderation."

By the time I went to bed that night, we had yet to talk about my family crisis. However, she had perfectly communicated empathy and understanding with her sheer presence. She knew what I needed and insisted that we wait for Uncle Larry to arrive in the morning to discuss my situation.

The next day began the very first conversation about my family crisis—a six-hour dialogue with Uncle Larry and his second wife, Aunt Denise. An all-day talking session was typical for us, during which you speak and they respond with deep care, wit, wisdom, and thought-provoking questions. We communicated about anything and everything—from divorce logistics to emotions to when and how we would tell our daughter, parents, and friends. Nana watched, listened, observed, and when asked, simply added, "Keep talking...you will figure it out." That was it—that was all she said. She did not talk the entire day, and yet, through her attention and support, had said as much as anyone else in the room.

By definition, communication is the transfer of information from one person to another. Nana successfully modeled non-verbal communication and I received her message loud and clear. She also reminded me of the value of voiced communication—speaking, writing, or even electronic. Talking to Nana and my aunt and uncle about this crisis made it real, an important step in getting across the bridge. Each time you explain what you are feeling and thinking, you help decrease the emotional charge of the crisis, which alleviates fear and promotes the healing process. Conversing also helps you to build rapport. By conveying your needs to the people who love you, you give them the opportunity to understand and support you. Talking about your situation, of course, does not come with a timeline, and only you can decide when you are ready.

As my vision was to remain a family, I wanted my husband to build the bridge with me and for the whole family to walk alongside one another. Nana taught us that the one thing that could undermine our family vision was to stop communicating. In any situation, communication takes two or more *good* people who are mindful of the words they choose when connecting with each other. I was fortunate that Case wanted to keep talking as much as

I did. And we talked and talked. No matter what, every night. My husband and I came home from work, went through our family routine, and then would return to talking about anything and everything. Our feelings. What we had learned in therapy. The resources we had found that day. Getting separate bank accounts. Anything. As long as we were talking, we were continuing across the bridge.

> *Everyone talks. Everyone communicates. But few connect. Those who do connect take their relationships, their work, and their lives to another level.*
> −John C. Maxwell

TIPS & TECHNIQUES

- ❖ Right before a difficult conversation, take a deep breath. *Breathe.* Listen. *Breathe.*

- ❖ Keep talking. It's all about relationships and the importance of human connections. Every individual has a purpose and every friendship has meaning.

- ❖ Choose your words carefully when communicating—words matter. Whether you are disappointed or angry, and especially in the heat of the moment, think about what you are about to say before you say it. Gather your thoughts and ask yourself, "Are the words I am about to say hurtful? What are less inflammatory words?"

- ❖ Be the first person to greet your family members and co-workers with a "good morning" smile—*every* morning. Smile to warm your heart, create connections, and help people feel appreciated.

❖ Pay attention to non-verbal cues. Position your hands in an open posture and don't fold your arms in a closed stance. Do not point your finger at the person. Allow personal space. Be aware of your tone of voice. Ask yourself, "Would I want the other person talking to me the way I am talking to them?"

❖ Listen to the other person's words. Actively listen. During a discussion, your role is to make sure you understand what is being communicated. Confirm what you heard by repeating and summarizing what you understand the individual is conveying. Start by asking, "Is this what I am hearing you say...?"

❖ Be mindful about with whom you discuss your situation, and when. Talking about your life circumstance makes it real. Communicate when YOU are ready. There is no timeline for telling others. When the time is right, remember, it is okay not to provide all the details and it is all right not to have all the answers. Every time you talk about your moment of crisis, it gets a little easier to tell your story. Communicate your thoughts, feelings, and beliefs, your vision for the future, and how the person can support *your* bridge.

❖ Act responsibly when communicating over social media. Think about who will be able to see what you have posted. Ask yourself, "Are there people I need to talk to *before* posting this on social media?" If verbal communication is too hard or not possible, send a written note or letter. Start by jotting down some ideas about what you want to convey. Draft the message. Pause and reflect on your words. Reread and edit the letter. Seeing your own words in writing, and then saying them out loud, helps you confirm your communication.

BRIDGE REFLECTION

Fire
   by Judy Sorum Brown

What makes a fire burn
is space between the logs,
a breathing space.
Too much of a good thing,
too many logs
packed in too tight
can douse the flames
almost as surely
as a pail of water would.
So building fires
requires attention
to the spaces in between,
as much as to the wood.
When we are able to build
open spaces
in the same way
we have learned
to pile on the logs,
then we can come to see how
it is fuel, and absence of the fuel
together, that make fire possible.
We only need to lay a log
lightly from time to time.
A fire
grows
simply because the space is there,
with openings
in which the flame
that knows just how it wants to burn
can find its way.

Brown, J.S. (2012). *The Art and Spirit of Leadership*. Bloomington, IN: Trafford Publishing. *(reproduced with permission)*

JOURNAL PROMPTS

The person I feel the most comfortable talking to is
  [who] , because...

_____

_____

_____

_____

_____

_____

_____

_____

I know I have been heard when...

_____

_____

_____

_____

_____

_____

_____

_____

_____

_____

What I want to talk about with my ___[who]___ is...

I communicate well when...

PRINCIPLE #5

Seek resources...Invest in the relationships that sustain you

Seek resources by investing the time to maintain relationships and make connections with friends, family, and community.

Focus on solutions.
—Nana

IN THE HEART OF MY FAMILY CRISIS, I wanted to believe I could get through it alone, that I had the tools and spirituality to carry me through. I wanted to think that I was acting with strength and courage, calmly and deliberately using my social work expertise to guide my journey to the other side of the bridge. I could clearly envision the *new* Corbett family. My bridge was being built using my knowledge and resources to get from point A to point B. I was nothing if not resourceful. I was dealing swiftly and promptly to find solutions to new situations and difficulties, yet even I couldn't "social work myself."

Taking actual steps across the bridge requires help beyond one's internal resources. It is interesting that people often find it difficult to accept the notion that asking for help is not a sign of weakness, but rather of might. Three interconnected spheres of influence offer the necessary resources to get you through your crisis: the individual, the family, and the community.

I looked to family for comfort and turned first to Nana, because she of all people would understand our vision to be a family. Always accepting and resourceful, Nana successfully blended three families and was the first person my cousin approached in the 1980s when he came out. It is a sign of her wisdom that throughout her lifetime she always seemed happy. I believe that her bridge to hope and healing was layered with contentment and understanding. I also called Uncle Larry, because he is encouraging and loving, and he's the best child and family social worker I will ever know.

I reached out to friends and friends who became family along the way for support. These long-standing, intense relationships evolved from both the good times and the difficult times. I trusted my dearest friend, Larissa, before any other, because we had known each other since 7th grade, shared the same values and spiritual beliefs, she had always been there for me for every difficult moment in middle-school, high-school, and college, and we lived in the same city. I fondly refer to her as my personal psychologist. The friends that have protected you and stood by you since childhood become your brothers and sisters by shared experiences and longevity. It is the history and familiarity within these relationships that sustain you, providing strength, hope, and energy. Even if there are gaps in the contact, the connections follow you throughout your life and you are able to just pick right back up where you left off.

I also went to my educational community for help in being an informed parent. My daughter's dad is gay, and Liz would eventually need to tell her friends why her parents were getting a divorce. I talked with the Director of Education at her religious school about how to explain homosexuality from a Jewish perspective to a fifth-grader. I contacted her teacher and administrator at her secular school to find out if they had experience with other families in our situation and to ask for their support and guidance. Community (work, social, school, religious, professional) is often a source of support that can be drawn upon as needed.

As a clinical social worker, I know mental health services are an essential resource in any crisis. However, as with many other mental health professionals, I tend to put others' needs before my own. It took a push from both Uncle Larry and Larissa for me to seek a therapist. I had to work through apprehension and stigma before I was reminded of how vital it was to find a confidential place to discuss my own feelings and thoughts.

My therapist recommended I attend a support group meeting with the Straight Spouse Network.[11] My initial reaction was to refuse. It sounded daunting and I didn't want to be categorized by this label, *straight spouse*. However, I understood clinically that being in a group made up of people *like* you—people facing a similar situation—may be a necessary resource. I did attend, and as a result, I connected with someone who instantly became my soul sister.

Despite all this, I still had to work through times of feeling alone and needed to be part of something bigger than myself for encouragement and inspiration along the way. Likeminded community is a resource toward building internal belonging. I turned to Hadassah,[12] an organization that believes Jewish values in action can repair the world [*Tikkun Olam*]. Pouring myself into volunteer work allowed me to give back to something bigger at a time when it was difficult to focus on myself. Being involved with a shared interest group can provide support, friendship, and connections, as well as give purpose and a sense of accomplishment.

It is important to turn to the *right* people for assistance. Dependable and positive people. If your family of origin, or the people you identify as family, are not supportive because they can't do it, won't do it, or don't accept you for who you are, then create your *own* family. These individuals and communities bring you comfort in moments of crisis and expect nothing in return. You have to reach out to someone—anyone—even when you *really* don't want to and especially during those foggy moments. Remember, you are loved, you are important, and you are special.

> *Trouble is a part of life, and if you don't share it,*
> *you don't give the people you love a chance to love you enough.*
> −Dinah Shore (via sign in therapist's office)

TIPS & TECHNIQUES

❖ When you are ready to find resources, take a deep breath. *Breathe.* Accept that it is okay to reach out for help—it is the ultimate sign of strength. *Breathe.* Let people help YOU. *Breathe.*

❖ Establish a network of supportive individuals who lift your spirits, feed your soul, make you laugh, and comfort you when you cry. Seek people that connect with you, provide encouragement, or are available when you are feeling lonely and alone. Ensure that you remain engaged with individuals who support your resiliency and *your* bridge.

❖ Surround yourself with solid, optimistic, considerate, and knowledgeable people who genuinely care about you. Define the type of person you envision being with you throughout your journey. Ask yourself, "Is the individual focused on my strengths, being supportive of my bridge, and encouraging healthy behaviors?" Seek out affirming people and limit your interaction with toxic people. If your family of origin or current friends are not able to help you or will not accept you for who you are because of their own capacity, insecurities, religious beliefs, or unresolved issues, create your own family. As a dear friend once said, "You are either in or you are in the way."

❖ Find a group of like-minded people, such as a support group of those who have experienced a similar life circumstance. You are not the *only* person who has dealt with this type of crisis. Believe you will find others and gather the strength and courage to contact them when you do. Invest the time to establish these new relationships, after all these are your sisters and brothers by circumstance and they will walk alongside of you as you build your bridge.

❖ Seek mental health therapy for a confidential place to discuss your concerns and feelings. Contact your health insurance provider, use your employer's Employee Assistance Program (EAP), or request referrals from friends and colleagues in the community. To help select the best therapist for you and your circumstance, consider these questions, "What type of treatment am I seeking? Am I looking for someone with a certain type of expertise? Would I be more comfortable talking with a man or a woman?" After the first few sessions, if there is not a connection and you do not feel comfortable, obtain another referral.

❖ Recognize the value of professionals and community organizations. Yoga specialists, massage therapists, clergy, and health care professionals can support, guide, and assist you along your journey. Choose something you care about that is bigger than yourself and volunteer. The mission and the people in the organization will provide community and give you a sense of belonging. Leverage the resources around you for help with specific requests, referrals, and suggestions for volunteer opportunities.

BRIDGE REFLECTION

My Hope for YOU
   by Becky S. Corbett

My *hope* is...YOU will have the strength to create a vision.

My *hope* is...even though your dreams may have been shattered, YOU will find the courage to create new, bigger dreams.

My *hope* is...YOU will take care of YOU.

My *hope* is...YOU will invest in the relationships that sustain YOU.

My *hope* is...YOU will ask for help, develop a support system, and accept when a friend loves you unconditionally, and becomes a ray of light in your cloud.

My *hope* is...YOU will have the determination to hold your head up high and the resiliency to keep moving forward.

My final *hope* is...YOU, your family, and community will know you are not alone.

JOURNAL PROMPTS

Supportive family and friends include...

_____

_____

_____

_____

_____

_____

_____

_____

_____

My friends and family support me when...

_____

_____

_____

_____

_____

_____

_____

_____

_____

_____

I am resourceful when...

I will seek something bigger than me by helping others to...

PRINCIPLE #6

Heal...Take care of you

Healing begins with taking care of yourself and connects mind, body, and spirit to feel whole.

Sit down, rest—take care of yourself.
—Nana

I N THIS MOMENT OF CRISIS, it was my spouse who came out, not me. Finding out that Case is gay started us on our journey, yet I had already spent two years feeling a distance in my marriage. For those two years I had pain from a herniated disc in my neck that no physical or medical treatment could make go away. The morning after my husband told me he is gay, that pain was gone. There is no question that the body and mind are inextricably linked.

Soon after that, I developed a short, wheezing cough every time I talked to a gay person and thought about my husband being gay. I wasn't sick and soon figured out that it was my subconscious telling me that I literally needed to stop and catch my breath. My mind was affecting my physical reactions. It was becoming clear that my physical, mental, and spiritual health were out of balance and I needed inner healing. Cultivating my mind, body, and spirit connection would be essential to emerge from this crisis and once more feel whole and at peace.

It is not uncommon for a person in any crisis to ignore self, throw out routines, and shift focus to others. Nevertheless, taking care of oneself during times of extreme stress is essential. Paying attention to my body's need for sleep, nutrition, and exercise was logically important. Yet pampering myself and remembering to smile was just as valuable to my healing process. Studies have shown that smiling may actually cause a happy sensation. While working with my therapist ensured I would focus on my mental health, humor was often just as powerful. When people asked, "Why are you getting a divorce? You seem so happy," my light-hearted answer was, "irreconcilable similarities." (Think about it—we both like men).

It is important to use all of your resources to reach harmony of mind, body and spirit, and doing so will be different for everyone. For example, healing spiritually can mean giving yourself a chance to dream or connect with your past. Another common path I often rely upon is turning to prayer. When I found myself questioning God, Cantor Larry provided comfort and spiritual wisdom. He, of course, was not able to give me *the answers*, but his response, "We find God in one another," reminded me that it was okay to ask others for help during my moments of crisis. Similarly, I need to be present for my family, friends, and community when they are going through difficult times.

I also drew on my Jewish traditions to guide my healing. The *Mi' She'Berach* is the Jewish prayer for healing. I found reassurance in reciting this prayer to myself when facing my most challenging moments. How would we remain a family? What would we tell our daughter? And so I would sing Debbie Friedman's lyrics, "May the source of strength who blessed the ones before us, help us find the courage to make our life a blessing."[13] Declaring to myself, "let the healing begin" which gave me strength and courage when I needed it most.

Throughout my journey, I tried many different methods to

foster my healing. Over time, I began to rely on those practices that repeatedly helped nurture me and my well-being. These involve a variety of approaches at different moments, such as writing letters, eating comfort food, and reminding myself to take a deep breath and breathe out. Ultimately, I cultivated my own *go-to* Healing Toolbox of these techniques that focus on healthy behaviors and positive solutions to guide my healing journeys. Each person's self-care needs are individual. Some of us need and desire to talk about our feelings, while others crave a physical release for anger, and others simply pray. It is important to recognize the practices that provide comfort as you strive toward creating your own personalized Healing Toolbox.

Social workers and other helping professionals place an emphasis on *taking care of yourself before you can take care of someone else*. During the initial moment of crisis, I dedicated myself to everyone else, largely putting my energy into supporting my husband in his coming-out process and into helping my daughter navigate *her* parents' divorce and her father's coming out. While being supportive and moving to action, I found I still had one hand holding on to a wide-open closet door ready to jump inside. It was pitch black and seemed like it would be so easy to stay for the rest of my life. I cried hysterically and then cried some more.

As I thought through the implications of what I was feeling, the one thing I realized was that I definitely didn't like being alone in the dark. That was an incentive to reach for the phone and call Uncle Larry. It doesn't matter if there was a spark of fear or just enough light that motivated me; I *needed* to make that one call. With care and understanding, he explained that he would have been surprised if I hadn't had a dark moment—or two or three. Then he reminded me how important it was to *take care of me.*

The hardest part is that a healing journey across the bridge is the responsibility of the person in crisis. There are probably as many barriers to self-care and nurturing the mind, body, and spirit as there are ways of practicing healing. I had to ask myself, borrowing the wisdom of Rabbi Hillel, *If I am not going to take care of me, who is?*[14] I was surrounded by friends, family, and community members who loved me and cared about me, however I had to be the one who gathered enough strength and courage to heal and grow.

Thriving in crisis requires the awareness and ability to actively bring the mind, body, and spirit into harmony. Everyone's healing timeline is different. Nana would frequently remind me, "You have done everything you can do for today—tomorrow is another day." This gave me the strength and courage to go to bed, count my blessings, get some sleep, and start back over the next day.

> *Allow yourself to rest. Your soul speaks to you in the quiet moments in between your thoughts.*
> –Anonymous

TIPS & TECHNIQUES

❖ When you want to connect your mind, body, and spirit, take a deep breath. *Breathe.* Say to yourself, "I will learn how to take care of my full self." *Breathe.*

❖ Focus on your physical, psychological, emotional, and spiritual health to feel whole again and at peace. Be open to new ideas that may not have previously seemed relevant. You are in a different time and place in your life. It is okay to keep it simple. Techniques can even be one-word instructions: sleep, walk, shop, relax, drink, eat, laugh.

❖ Discover your *Healing Place*—a place you call home, where you feel most at peace, or have full sense of harmony. Consider the five senses and ask yourself, "What do I see? What do I smell? What do I hear? What can I taste? How does it feel to be in *this place*?" Visit or close your eyes and envision something that brings you peace and calms you—perhaps a sunset or sunrise, a particular beach, lake, waterfall, or mountain, a painting, drawing, or photograph that makes you smile.

❖ Find strength and healing in your religion and spirituality. Ask yourself, "When do I turn to God, a Biblical verse, or a place of worship? Do I pray and hold my faith close during good times, a loss or a tragedy, a life-cycle event? What lifts my spirits?" Consider taking a yoga class, learning how to meditate, and engaging in mindfulness.

❖ Listen to music, sing, dance, or play a musical instrument. Engage with the sounds, melodies, and words that speak to your soul. Sing softly or loudly. Turn on your favorite song— the one that makes you feel good. Belt it out again and again— one more time. Dance to music that makes you feel alive.

❖ Pause and reflect. Allow yourself time for your heart to connect with your mind and body and process how you are thinking and feeling. If it seems that you can't breathe, create some space. It *is* possible to feel overwhelmed and smothered by the very people who are there to support you.

❖ Because the fog may become extremely dense, and you may experience moments of deep despair and loneliness, trust others and reach out, even when you don't want to. In those dark moments, tell someone—anyone.

❖ Have a good cathartic cry—a nonsensical, yet useful, let-it-out cry that leaves your eyes bloodshot and puffy. The cry that makes you feel like you can't breathe, the one that leaves you empty and ready to start again.

❖ As Nana always said, "Everything in moderation"—that is how she took care of herself. Have *one* drink, in celebration or to relax. Eat some comfort food, but don't finish the *whole* pie. It is okay to feel hurt and upset and express your anger, just not for too long. Avoid getting stuck in any one state.

❖ Determine what is needed to take care of yourself. Identify what may motivate or who might inspire you to move to action. Learn to understand yourself and become a stronger and knowledgeable you. Ask yourself, "Who am I when I am alone? What do I do? What do I enjoy? How do I behave? What do I read? What nourishes my soul?" Engage in *me* time—carve out periods by yourself, for yourself, and with yourself. After all, *self-care starts with me.* Some examples include:

  ⅄ Politely decline invitations to events you feel you are not ready to attend.

  ⅄ Binge watch television shows and movies and don't forget the popcorn.

  ⅄ Purchase one thing you would not have typically bought for yourself.

  ⅄ Escape and pamper yourself—get a massage, style your hair differently, enjoy a manicure/pedicure.

  ⅄ Plan a retreat—stay near or go far, take a vacation or a stay-cation, and tell everyone that you went away.

  ⅄ Give some extra attention to a pet in your life or provide kindness to an animal in need.

  ⅄ Implement a tech-wellness plan. For a self-defined amount of time, shut down all of your technical devices and social media.

  ⅄ Take up a hobby for pleasure and relaxation. Engage in activities you enjoy and look forward to doing. From drawing and painting to cooking to fishing to gardening to reading, writing, and scrapbooking—the possibilities are endless.

BRIDGE REFLECTION

There is Hope
  by Rabbi David Paskin

There is hope, there is healing.
There is peace and there is blessing.

When the waters are wide...and you...
Cannot reach the other side
Should your courage run dry...

What you try to endure
When the future's unsure
Believe there's something more...

There is hope, there is healing.
There is peace and there is blessing.

Paskin, D. (2016). There is hope. www.davidpaskin.com. *(reproduced with permission)*

JOURNAL PROMPTS

My body reacts to stress by...

I take care of myself by...

An inspirational quote, poem, or prayer that inspires me to take care of ME is...

_____

_____

_____

_____

_____

_____

_____

_____

Mind, body, and spirit techniques I will use in a moment of crisis include...

_____

_____

_____

_____

_____

_____

_____

_____

_____

_____

PRINCIPLE #7

Accept, adjust, and affirm...
Life moves forward

Shifting from acceptance to adjustment to affirmation helps you to keep moving forward.

> *As time goes by, your perspective evolves.*
> —Nana

WHILE MY HUSBAND WAS COMING OUT OF THE CLOSET, I often grappled with retreating into my own closet. I wanted to hide from him, our daughter, and the world. Of course, I knew that pretending this all wasn't happening would not make it go away. And being angry, resentful, and withdrawn from life would most certainly keep me from moving forward. I had to move past the revelation and accept my husband for who he is, adjust to the fact that I was going to be divorced, and realize that it was up to me to lead myself and my family across the bridge. Acceptance is coming to terms with the situation that actually happened, not disregarding it or the hurt.

Resiliency—the capacity to recover quickly from difficulties—will determine just how easily one accepts an unexpected situation and adjusts one's life and behavior to the new circumstances. Even when unhappy, I most often accept that I can't change what has happened and swiftly move to action. I had to ask myself, "What did I need to adjust in my life or in my mind to adapt to my new situation?" To fully accept my soon-to-be former husband as a gay man, I not only had to acknowledge his homosexuality, but adjust to the unfamiliar territory of a new community with different prejudices and even its own vocabulary. This involved educating myself about the gay community and the coming-out process, so I could understand what my husband was experiencing. To move forward as a divorced woman, simply seeking out single female friends helped me acclimate to this unfamiliar circumstance.

Self-doubt can amplify difficulties in healing from a life-changing moment. Questioning yourself, your perceived worth, self-integrity, or even your prior decisions can bring your healing journey to an abrupt halt. One well-researched approach to dealing with crisis is self-affirmation. Positive statements about oneself have been shown to enable the acceptance of a disruptive event and facilitate adaptation. Self-affirmation can help you cope through the *woulda, coulda, shoulda* and is associated with increased well-being.

With a deep internal need to thrive, I knew that surviving wasn't enough. My affirmation journey needed to go beyond accepting that my husband is gay. I wanted to understand what Case was going through and affirm the entire gay community. I didn't want to just get a divorce; I wanted to have the divorce that mattered. Healing meant learning something along the way and walking my family across the bridge. Of course, thriving takes that one step further.

God grant me the serenity to accept the things I cannot change;
Courage to change the things I can;
And wisdom to know the difference.
—Reinhold Niebuhr

TIPS & TECHNIQUES

- ❖ When moving forward, take a deep breath. *Breathe.* Repeat this mantra, "I want to move forward. I can move forward. I will move forward. I am moving forward." *Breathe.*

- ❖ Take initiative. Choose resiliency by making the decision to accept, affirm, and adjust to your life circumstance.

- ❖ Give yourself time to work through the emotions surrounding loss and grief—denial, anger, bargaining, depression, and acceptance. Regardless of what you have lost, be aware that loss is loss. Whether you are mourning the loss of a loved one, a marriage, or life as you once knew it, healing is a process. Grief comes in waves and mourning takes time. It ebbs and flows. New losses may bring up old losses. There is no one right way to grieve or specific period of time to mourn.

- ❖ Be the individual who says *something* and doesn't ignore uncomfortable truths.

- ❖ Put yourself in the other person's shoes and try to see the situation from their point of view. Don't assume you know someone or their story. Be present without judgment and choose to be the one who listens. If you feel uncomfortable at first, imagine what the other person may be thinking and feeling.

- ❖ Go back to the familiar. Reach out to others, near and far, reconnect with a childhood friend or long-lost family member, and reminisce about the good old days. Look at sentimental photos and handmade scrapbooks, watch videos, read journals and school papers, and to appreciate your past, go through your "life box."

❖ Welcome and embrace someone new. When someone reaches out to you and you are in a position to listen, do so—take the phone call, respond to the email, or answer the text. Even though you may never fully understand what you did for that individual, in that moment it is valuable to just be available.

❖ Love with your whole heart, take a little risk, care immensely, change your attitude, and look at the situation from a fresh perspective. When you find yourself stuck, create a diversion and get some fresh air. Believe you can clear your head, return to center, and keep moving forward.

BRIDGE REFLECTION

Bat Mitzvah Prayer for Liz
   by Becky S. Corbett and James C. Corbett

As we have watched you grow, it has appeared to us that many of your accomplishments come naturally to you.
We want to say a few words to you today to help you realize how much you have, and how much you have to give to others.

You have been loved, may you show your love to others.
You are confident, may you inspire others to soar.
You are bright, may you share your knowledge.
You are tall, may you strive to be looked up to.

You have dreamt, may you express hope to others.
You are generous, may you continue to care.
You have led, may you allow others to show you new ways.
You have inherited much from those that came before you, may you continue to embrace all that we call family.

Today, you have become a Bat Mitzvah. May you always cherish the moments when you learned acceptance and observed affirmation of all people as a foundation for a bright future.

In the name of Sarah, Rebecca, Rachel, Leah, blessed is our daughter.

Amen.

Bat Mitzvah is a lifecycle event celebrated when a Jewish girl turns 12 years old and assumes her own responsibility for Jewish ritual law, tradition, and ethics, and has all the rights and obligations of a Jewish adult.

JOURNAL PROMPTS

A time in my life when I exhibited resiliency was...

_____

_____

_____

_____

_____

_____

_____

_____

In this moment, the one thing I can change is...

_____

_____

_____

_____

_____

_____

_____

_____

In this life circumstance, the one thing I cannot change but can adapt to is...

_____

_____

_____

_____

_____

_____

_____

_____

_____

I will accept, adjust to, and affirm this life-changing moment because...

_____

_____

_____

_____

_____

_____

_____

_____

_____

_____

PRINCIPLE #8

Forgive...Let go

Forgiveness is an inside effort and letting go is an opportunity for internal peace.

> *Forgiveness creates serenity.*
> —Nana

MY HUSBAND DID NOTHING TO PURPOSELY HARM ME, but I was hurt. Do I really need to forgive him? Even though not deliberate, Case's coming out made me face feelings of anger, embarrassment, and sadness. I was mad about getting divorced, about my husband not knowing he is gay when we married, and at a world that didn't allow him to be true. These negative emotions were painful, and I had a broken heart and a broken spirit.

Anger is a normal response to a hurtful situation and if unresolved, can lead to destructive behaviors and thoughts, even resulting in physical and mental health issues. To heal, you need to go beyond simply releasing anger and actively free *yourself* from holding on to the negative emotions you have attached to a past wrongdoing. Forgiveness is a deeply personal and deliberate act of letting go—it has little to do with the other person. Additionally, forgiveness is not condoning a hurtful action, forgetting the wrong, or ignoring that there might be consequences.

Forgiveness takes time and is a process. Letting go requires a degree of self-esteem and the capacity to empathize in order to replace the harmful emotions with understanding and compassion. I could forgive my husband because, although his coming out threw our family into crisis, I did not blame him for being gay in a world that isn't yet fully accepting. Neither of us were aware that he was gay when we met and married. I also had to let go of criticizing myself for my previous unawareness. One can only act according to the information available at the moment.

Forgiveness is an inside effort and does mean different things to different people. Each individual has to define what to let go. I not only had to let go of what was and what could have been in my life, but also forgive myself for being human. To overcome the hurtful situation, I had to let go of blame and resentment about what had happened and release the impact that my husband's coming out and our pending divorce was having on my life. The goal of forgiveness is to bring about a sense of peace and facilitate healing, which helps you to move forward. For me, forgiving allowed me to imagine my world on the other side of the bridge. It meant going to a restaurant and movie by myself, and eventually seeing other men. Forgiveness and letting go allows you to live in peace.

It's one of the greatest gifts you can give yourself, to forgive.
Forgive everybody.
−Maya Angelou

TIPS & TECHNIQUES

❖ When forgiving, take a deep breath. *Breathe.* Let go. *Breathe.* Forgive and let it all go. *Breathe.*

❖ Seek out constructive ways to release negative emotions and the tension you feel. Engage in physical activity. Cry until you feel depleted. Secure a spot to scream as loud as you can at the top of your lungs. Then scream LOUDER.

❖ Give yourself time to forgive—it is a process. What you feel and believe in the initial moment of crisis is probably not what you will be feeling and thinking weeks, months, and years down the road.

❖ Create the space to meditate, pray, or reflect. Ask yourself, "What must I do to forgive the people and the circumstances in this moment of crisis? What is one thing I can do for me to bring about inner peace?"

❖ Let go of anger and resentment as quickly as possible. It is okay to be the first person to say, "I'm sorry." When appropriate, give people a second and even a third chance. Avoid regrets.

❖ To gain focus when you are struggling to let go of a grudge, go for a long ride—by car, bike, train, boat, or horseback.

❖ Be patient. Just because you may want to discuss forgiveness, the other person may not be ready. Give the individual time and space. Continue with your own forgiveness and let go. Remain positive and never lose hope that you will have the opportunity to communicate.

❖ Keep a little piece of you, to YOU. There are private thoughts, feelings, and actions that you may never share with other people. It is okay to hold on to these for yourself.

BRIDGE REFLECTION

The Bridge
   by Rabbi Karyn K. Kadar

Forgiveness is a path to be walked.
There are steps along the way:
loss, anger, acceptance, learning,
forgiveness, restoration.

And along the way, you will come upon a bridge.
When you step upon it, it will carry you,
support you, connect you to another side of life,
a side waiting to be discovered.

Forgiveness is a perpetual journey.
There are many bridge crossings.
Each restores a bit more of what you have lost.

Begin.

Kadar, K.K. (2007). The bridge. In *The bridge to forgiveness: Stories and prayers for finding God and restoring wholeness*. pg 1. Nashville, TN: Jewish Lights Publishing. (*reproduced with permission*)

JOURNAL PROMPTS

When I hold on to anger and resentment, it...

Full peace and harmony look and feel like...

I will forgive __[who]__ for __[what]__ because...

My final "let go" for this life circumstance will be...

PRINCIPLE #9

Express gratitude...
Count your blessings

Gratitude is sincerely expressing your thoughtful appreciation. Counting your blessings encourages you to pause and be thankful.

> *I am thankful for my three families.*
> —Nana

T**HE EXPRESSION OF GRATITUDE IS AN ACT OF KINDNESS** for recognizing someone's value. When life is going well, it is easy to feel grateful. My husband agreed to build the *new* Corbett family with me. We established a new friendship and happily attended our daughter's school meetings and family functions together. It was natural to express my gratitude after each event, and I made sure Case received a sincere note via email or text.

During times of crisis, having the wherewithal to appreciate those around you might seem insurmountable. How can one be grateful during the most difficult times? Those days I felt angry at Case, my steps across the bridge got tripped up, or I slipped back into the fog, I did not feel particularly gracious. However, during these tough periods, I took the time to appreciate what I did have. I counted my blessings: #1—my soon-to-be former husband was still my friend, #2—our daughter wasn't losing a father or a mother, and #3—our family was physically healthy. This created hope and maintained our connection. It was essential for me to choose to be grateful and to identify what is good in my life. Counting my blessings provided me with the opportunity to pause, reflect, and be thankful.

Regularly communicating gratitude has been shown to increase mental and physical health, in addition to boosting overall resilience and enhancing one's response to a life circumstance. Thanking someone gives you the opportunity to step outside of a difficult situation and pay attention to what truly matters. The fundamental mindset of thankfulness extends beyond the moment of crisis, builds a positive outlook, increases your ability to see a situation in a new light, and lets the person know how they helped you. A grateful perspective on life promotes reflection and shifts attention from difficult circumstances to beneficial ones.

When you genuinely thank the people who matter, it creates enthusiasm, for both you and the individual, and strengthens your relationship. I often felt it was critical for *my* healing journey to express gratitude to the individuals that were present and there for our family. As we kept moving forward, I constantly informed the people who sustained me how much I cared for them. Make a conscious choice to show your appreciation to the family, friends, and communities that have supported *your* bridge to hope and healing.

Gratitude makes sense of our past, brings peace for today,
and creates a vision for tomorrow.
—Melody Beattie

TIPS & TECHNIQUES

* Right before you express gratitude, take a deep breath. *Breathe.* Count your blessings. *Breathe* again.

* Be grateful for YOU—you *are* living your core values and being your bridge.

* Count your blessings every day, before you go to sleep and when you wake up in the morning. Think of all the aspects of your life that define you. List everything you are thankful for.

* Show your sincere appreciation to another and graciously express your gratitude. Write a handwritten thank-you note, pick up the telephone and make a call, send a card in the mail, type an email or text, publicly thank an individual over social media, or buy the person a little gift. To demonstrate sincerity, be specific about why you are acknowledging the person.

* Be a friend to someone experiencing a moment of crisis. As a dear friend eloquently said, "It's what you do." It feels good and that person might be there for you in return. Helping someone in need takes your mind off your own fears and troubles. Welcome the individual with a reassuring smile, be a sounding board or problem-solver, or simply sit quietly together. Listen and check on them—often.

* Create a world in which everyone you come into contact with, on any given day, makes eye contact with you, acknowledges your presence, and genuinely means, "Have a nice day."

BRIDGE REFLECTION

Gratitude in Action
by Becky S. Corbett

A heart-felt, genuine thank you to those who have been a part of building the multiple bridges in my life. Some of you were there for moments and some have been there for each step, across every bridge.

To my *mishpachah* [family]; life-long childhood, camp, middle-school, high-school, and college friends; sorority sisters; friends who have become family along the way; educators; spiritual community; professional colleagues; attorneys; advisors and mentors; fellow volunteers; sisters and brothers by circumstance; brothers and sisters by shared experiences and longevity; beta readers and book editors; and the Bridge creative, programming, and legal team—I am forever grateful for your love, warmth, and friendship.

And finally, to the *new* Corbett Family. Case—for giving me the wings to fly; Liz—for always being my sunshine; and Hugh—for becoming family.

All of YOU were and continue to provide me with the strength and courage to live my dreams. Thank you for walking alongside me throughout my journey across *The Bridge to Hope & Healing*®. When I count my blessings, I count all of you, twice.

JOURNAL PROMPTS

When someone genuinely thanks me, I feel...

I will express my sincere gratitude to __[who]__,
for __[what]__, by __[date]__ ...

When I reflect on the moment of crisis that helped me
become the person I am today, I am grateful for...

_____

_____

_____

_____

_____

_____

_____

_____

_____

I count my blessings when...

_____

_____

_____

_____

_____

_____

_____

_____

_____

_____

_____

_____

EPILOGUE

From the other side of the bridge

Never forget where you came from.
−The value my daddy taught me

Everything happens for a reason.
−The wisdom my mama instilled in me

I T TOOK YEARS TO HAVE MY FEET FIRMLY PLANTED enough on the other side of the bridge to complete this book. Through patches of fog, circumstances that made me stumble, as well as moments that kept me moving forward, we did achieve my vision—we are a family. It is most beautifully expressed in our daughter Liz's college application essay that she wrote at the age of 17: "My parents are the two strongest people and closest friends I have known and will ever know. Together, my mother, father, and stepfather have raised me to be the independent, mature, strong-willed and well-rounded young woman that I am. My family is weird but also normal, and I will be forever grateful to have experienced such diversity in my childhood."[15]

Twelve years after learning that my husband is gay, I have mourned. I have cried. I have laughed. I have lived. I have made mistakes. I mourned the loss of my marriage and traditional home. I cried again and I laughed again. Through it all, life moved forward. I started my own company, Case married Hugh, and Liz graduated from college Summa Cum Laude with two degrees. There were occasions and holidays that we all spent together and times when we simply did our own thing. It wasn't enough for me to just have the vision. I like to say that I built the bridge, but actually everyone else had to choose to walk across it. And they did. It would be fair to say we built the bridge together. I was truly humbled when Hugh wrote me a personal thank-you note for welcoming him into my life wholly and without condition. For me, it confirmed his love for my former husband and our daughter.

Looking back over the bridge, we thrived, and there are many reasons why. I naturally look inward, have the ability to set a vision, and use my innate and acquired resources—my strength and courage, spirituality, and social work training. Those are part of the many aspects of my life that define me, not just my marriage. This life circumstance isn't about my husband coming out, it is actually a journey about *me*—*my* mental health and *my* personal growth. Although I was surrounded by friends, family, and community members who loved me and cared about me, I had to be the one to gather enough strength and courage to take the first step and reach out for help. It actually doesn't matter which came first—the fog lifting just enough for me to begin to envision the storm passing, the sun coming out, a beautiful rainbow ascending, and then a crystal-clear sky prevailing—or a dark, painful moment that eventually helped me realize that peace comes from within. Regardless, I am responsible for my own healing.

When I think back on the younger version of myself, I have no regrets. Just shy of my 22nd birthday, on September 28, 1991, I walked down that long aisle with my daddy at Temple Sinai in New Orleans, to greet my husband under the *chuppah* [wedding canopy]. At that time in my life, I did the right thing and would still do it all over again in a heartbeat.

In full transparency, I am unsure if one ever fully recovers from moments of crisis experienced throughout a lifetime. However, I do know this—you can change your outlook, *choose* to build a bridge to hope and healing, and grow into the next version of yourself. Without my journey, we would not have the daughter we do, and I would have never become the person I am today.

Do I still have some difficult moments? You bet I do. Every past crisis is like a movie reel playing in my head. And when I need to, I give myself the gift of a heartfelt, gut-wrenching cry. I may even read an old journal entry, look through some photos, or listen to a song that reminds me of what was. Then I look in the mirror and remind myself—with compassion and passion—*We did build our bridge to hope and healing...we are the new Corbett family.*

Nana died at the end of 2016[16] the way she wanted—peacefully. During her *shiva* [mourning rituals], I took the opportunity to reflect on her influence in creating our family philosophy. Family is family—and our daughter Liz still has a mother and father. In this moment, I realized the gift of my Nana Banana as my mentor through all of my family crises. She inspired me to think beyond conventional boundaries and was always just a telephone call away.

A year later, the discovery of a basal cell on my head and the fear triggered by the possibility of skin cancer threw me into a new fog. While waiting for the results, I instinctively found myself going back to each of the strategies Nana inspired. Leaning on that guidance, I essentially built another bridge along a new hope and healing journey. I tested the concepts that I had begun to develop. Although I had not yet formulated them in writing, I was living the 9 Principles. And they worked. As the doctor explained what a basal cell was—I went into a fog—all I heard was skin *cancer*. Show strength and courage—learn about the treatment protocols. Hope—the fog will lift. Seek resources—contact a knowledgeable colleague. Take care of me—listen to Cantor Larry's CD and sing *Heal Us Now*.[17] Count my blessings—the basal cell was completely removed and was benign. Accept, adjust, and affirm—change my behaviors in the sun.

As friends, family members, and colleagues continued to reach out to me during their moments of crisis, I began to recognize that other individuals and communities lacked their own resources and could benefit from what I was composing. Nana would certainly have agreed that you have the power to learn from a life circumstance, transform any difficult situation into a growth opportunity, and thrive throughout your life journey. For me, thriving is building something from the moment of crisis and making a difference in someone else's life.

To honor my Nana Banana, Frances Wallach Weissberger Schwartz, *z"l* [may her memory forever be a blessing], I created *The Bridge to Hope & Healing*®.

Final Journal Prompts

Now that you have read each Principle and have worked through the Tips & Techniques, Bridge Reflections, and Journal Prompts, you are ready to acknowledge that this moment of crisis does not define you. Choose to turn your hope and healing pursuit into a growth journey. Apply the concepts that most resonate with you and create a life-long Healing Toolbox. Be flexible—repeat the same techniques for the same Principle multiple times or try new ones to navigate your next life circumstance.

These final Journal Prompts will help you look back over your bridge, count your blessings, and celebrate how far you have come. Congratulations—you have built your bridge to hope and healing.

JOURNAL PROMPTS

Circumstances will continue to change in my life—the children will grow up, my parents and grandparents will age, and others may disappoint me. I will continue to move forward by...

Standing on the other side of my bridge:
I look back, reflect, and realize...

The milestones that have helped me become the person
I am today are...

_____
_____
_____
_____
_____
_____
_____
_____
_____
_____

When I experience another moment of crisis, I will
survive and thrive through that life circumstance and
build another bridge to hope and healing because...

_____
_____
_____
_____
_____
_____
_____
_____
_____

ACKNOWLEDGEMENT

Dear Liz,

I have been telling our friends and family for years, what took me an entire book to write, you captured in a one-page college essay.[15] As you noted about Nana, she taught us that family is everything. We are so fortunate to have had her in our lives—she passed on an amazing legacy.

Thank YOU for being the most amazing daughter. It is an honor to be your mommy, friend, and sorority sister.[18] You will always be my sunshine.

> *L'Dor V'Dor* [from generation to generation],
> may you go from strength to strength
> and have the courage to build a
> bridge to hope & healing in times of need.

I love you,

Mommy

NOTES

[1] Henry S. Jacobs Camp (www.jacobscamp.org) is the Reform Jewish summer camp in Utica, Mississippi which serves children from the Deep South. Jacobs Camp is part of the Union for Reform Judaism (www.urj.org) family of camps and youth programs.

[2] Sigma Delta Tau (SDT) (www.sigmadeltatau.org) is a national sorority founded in 1917. As a member of the National Panhellenic Conference, SDT is committed to empowering women through scholarship, service, sisterhood, and leadership.

[3] See Appendix for full text of "The Letter."

[4] Clark, E.J., & Hoffler, E.F. (Eds.). (2014). *Hope matters: The power of social work*. Washington, DC: NASW Press.

[5] Clark, E.J. (2017). *Choose hope (always choose hope)*. Murrells Inlet, SC: Covenant Books.

[6] Buxton, A. (1994). *The other side of the closet: The coming-out crisis for straight spouses and families*. New York, NY: J. Wiley.

[7] Lambda Legal (www.lambdalegal.org) was founded in 1973 as the nation's first legal organization dedicated to achieving full equality for lesbian and gay people. Their legal, educational, and advocacy work touches nearly every aspect of life for lesbians, gay men, bisexuals, transgender people, and people living with HIV.

[8] The Human Rights Campaign (HRC) (www.hrc.org) is the largest national lesbian, gay, bisexual, transgender and queer (LGBTQ) civil rights organization. HRC envisions a world where LGBTQ people are ensured of their basic equal rights and can be open, honest, and safe at home, at work, and in the community.

[9] Passover is the springtime Jewish festival that commemorates the liberation of the Israelites from Egyptian slavery more than 3,000 years ago.

[10] Passover Seder is a Jewish ceremonial dinner, held the first night or first two nights of the Holiday of Freedom, which includes a ritual service to recount the Israelites' exodus from Egyptian slavery.

[11] The Straight Spouse Network (SSN) (www.straightspouse.org) is an international organization that provides personal, confidential support, and information to heterosexual spouses/partners of gay, lesbian, bisexual, or transgender mates and mixed-orientation or transgender/non-transgender couples. SSN serves straight spouses, post-disclosure couples, families, and the community.

[12] Hadassah is The Women's Zionist Organization of America (www.hadassah.org) connecting Jewish women and empowering them to effect change through advocacy, advancing health and well-being, and support of Israel.

[13] Friedman, D. (1988). *Mi Shebeirach.* Schaumburg, IL: Transcontinental Music Publications.

[14] Borrowed from, "If I am not for myself, who will be for me?" Hillel the Elder. Pirkei Avot, Ethics of the Fathers, 1:14.

[15] See Appendix for full text of "Liz's College Essay."

[16] See Appendix for full text of "Nana's Eulogy."

[17] Sher, L. (2002). *Heal us now.* Schaumburg, IL: Transcontinental Music Publications.

[18] When Becky's daughter Liz joined Sigma Delta Tau, they became sorority sisters and Becky passed on to Liz the sorority pin originally worn by her maternal great-grandmother, Dada, also a sister.

BECKY'S BOOKSHELF

The list of books that Becky read to help build her
bridge to hope and healing.

Ahrons, C. (1994). *The good divorce: Keeping your family together when your marriage comes apart.* New York, NY: HarperCollins.

Beattie, M. (1990). *The language of letting go.* Center City, MN: Hazelden Foundation.

Brown, B. (2012). *Daring greatly.* New York, NY: Penguin Random House.

Buxton, A. (1994). *The other side of the closet: The coming-out crisis for straight spouses and families.* New York, NY: Wiley.

Canfield, J., & Hansen, M. (2005). *Chicken soup for the recovering soul: Daily inspirations.* Deerfield Beach, FL: Health Communications.

Cutler, H. with His Holiness the Dalai Lama. (1998). *The art of happiness: A handbook for living.* New York, NY: Riverhead Books.

Frankl, V. (2006). *Man's search for meaning.* Boston, MA: Beacon Press.

Gochros, J.S. (1989). *When husbands come out of the closet.* New York, NY: Harrington Park Press.

Grever, C. (2001). *My husband is gay: A woman's guide to surviving the crisis.* Toronto, ON: The Crossing Press.

Kaye, B. (2006). *Straight wives, shattered lives. Stories of women with gay husbands.* Martinsville, IN: Airleaf Publishing.

Kedar, K.D. (1999). *God whispers: Stories of the soul, lessons of the heart.* Nashville, TN: Jewish Lights Publishing.

Kedar, K.D. (2001). *Our dance with God.* Nashville, TN: Jewish Lights Publishing.

Kedar, K.D. (2007). *The bridge to forgiveness: Stories and prayers for finding God and restoring wholeness.* Nashville, TN: Jewish Lights Publishing.

Kirshenbaum, M. (2004). *Everything happens for a reason: Finding the true meaning of the events in our lives.* New York, NY: Harmony Books.

Komuves, L.B.C. (2006). *Silent sagas, unsung sorrows. Heterosexual wife, homosexual husband.* New York, NY: iUniverse.

Kushner, H. (1981). *When bad things happen to good people.* New York, NY: Schocken Books.

Kushner, H. (2006). *Overcoming life's disappointments.* New York, NY: Knopf Publishers.

Maxwell, J. (2010). *Everyone communicates, few connect.* Nashville, TN: Thomas Nelson.

Maxwell, J. (2012). *The 15 invaluable laws of growth.* New York, NY: Center Street.

Mogel, W. (2001). *The blessing of a skinned knee: Using Jewish teachings to raise self-reliant children.* New York, NY: Scribner.

Moore, S., & Bernstein, R.F. (1996). *A journal of healing: Writing through pain and illness.* New York, NY: Doubleday.

Netter, P. (2002). *Divorce is a mitzvah: A practical guide to finding wholeness and holiness when your marriage dies.* Nashville, TN: Jewish Lights Publishing.

Pagels, D. (2013). *The next chapter of your life.* Boulder, CO: Blue Mountain Press.

Ricci, I. (1997). *Mom's house, dad's house: Making two homes for your child.* New York, NY: Fireside.

Sarton, M. (1973). *Journal of a solitude.* New York, NY: Norton.

Snow, J.E. (2004). *How it feels to have a gay or lesbian parent: A book by kids for kids of all ages.* Binghamton, NY: Harrington Park Press.

Stoddard, A. (1990). *Gift of a letter.* New York, NY: Doubleday.

Tuerk, C. (2012). *Mom knows: Reflections on love, gay pride, and taking action.* Washington, DC: Catherine Tuerk.

White, M. (1994). *Stranger at the gate: To be gay and Christian in America.* New York, NY: Simon & Schuster.

APPENDIX

THE LETTER

October 30, 2006

Dear Casey:

   I thought it was best to sit down and write you a letter. My hope is that it will provide you with some information that I have been "holding back" for a few years.

   I have always said, "I married my best friend." And how true that is. We do have fun together. Ever since our honeymoon in Costa Rica, I look forward to our travel. We seem to have created a rhythm over the years that just "feels" right. We have financially and emotionally supported each other as we have both grown our careers. And I think we talk about everything except "one" thing...

   This is the difficult part. Sharing my private thoughts about my physical needs. I think we can both admit that we have not been direct with each other about our thoughts and feelings—and my suggestion to us is that we begin this most intimate dialogue. (And I do recognize how different we are in our approaches to tough topics.)

   Case—I have cried myself to sleep too many nights in the last few years. And I realize how "emotional" I will be getting this out on the table. So, I decided to write the letter to try to communicate—initially in writing. It will also give you time to think about what I am saying.

Why have I cried? Because I have feared you were no longer attracted to me or that you were having an affair—and recently my imagination and thoughts have just gotten out of control. And I need to just ask you—what's going on—what are you thinking and feeling?

Last week I woke up on Wednesday morning at 5am. I went downstairs and just cried. Hysterically. I realized that this time, I can't just "let it go." You are TOO important to me. We have been married 15 years and I really want to grow old with you. Almost everything is good about "us." Yeah—we have our "moments," but for as long as I can remember, we have been "compatible." From parenting styles to house choices (except the pink dining room has got to go).

Case—I know how emotional I am—remember I have to live with me. I also believe our physical needs are different. My concern is that we have both made some assumptions and that it is time to be more open with each other.

So here goes...what I want you to know is that I am lonely. I want and need to come home at the end of the workday and know that we are there for each other mentally and physically. What physical means—we both need to agree on.

Last Sunday night it was a "typical" Becky and Casey conversation. Schedule for the week, work/career advice, etc. And then I asked the question about you being attracted to me. It wasn't the words that troubled me. It was the entire response. But I didn't push, and I hoped I conveyed that "I was here." What I didn't do was go the next step and tell you how I have really felt—hurt, angry, scared, and confused—all about our physical relationship.

When I went to bed that night, I "felt" better because the elephant in the room had been recognized. I thought, give him some space, but that plan worked for 48 hours. When I woke up at 5am on Wednesday, I went downstairs. I could barely breathe. Literally. I was crying so hard. I thought, I can't live like this anymore. What should I do? RUN? Wake you up to yell or talk? But I did what I do best—I went to work, once again. And I came home to my family. Because this is where I want to be.

Please know that I recognize this is not easy on either of us. We have our own intimate/physical thoughts and needs. I am scared and feel "uncomfortable" opening up to you on this topic—because it is so private—but Case, I can't keep doing this. It's not fair to either one of us. This isn't just about you—it's also about me and about us. And for me, I don't want to keep living with this physical distance between us.

My goal in giving you this letter is to be "direct" and ask you to work on this part of our marriage together. I believe we both play a role in what has happened over the years. I re-read the letter you sent me before we got married (of course I have it). The letter is about how we both view money. The experts say the two big topics in a marriage are sex and money. We have come a long way with our philosophy on finances, from growing our personal wealth to teaching Liz the value of money. We even share similar religious views—your choice to convert to Judaism and planning our family trip to Israel.

So now I am asking "us" to work on the physical side of our marriage. I want both of us to be "as comfortable" as we can be for the next discussion. Write me back and/or let's agree on the time and location in the next few weeks. I am okay with it just being the two of us for this next step and am open to a third-party being present. Case, I'm NOW asking DIRECTLY—for you to talk to me. I am suggesting we meet each other as close to half way as we can at this time in our own private thoughts. I don't mean a 4-hour lunch at Bonefish discussing our feelings (my preference) or a 5-minute conversation in front of the TV and laptop (your preference). I hope you are smiling.

I want us to do what the Corbetts do best. Let's be creative, open to what the other has to say, and agree on how to move forward—together.

There is not a "good" time to open this dialogue. We both have a full life—careers, volunteer work (we're even both serving as "President" for two different organizations), obsessions (biking and shopping for motivational signs), and of course our shared responsibility in raising the most incredible daughter—she is who she is today because of both of us.

And, I am asking us—both of us—to put this "first" over the next several months.

As I always have and I always will—I love you!
Becky

LIZ'S COLLEGE ESSAY

Fall 2013

I feel most content when I am sitting at home on my perfectly soft, coffee-colored couch because I am five feet away from my true love, my hobby, my passion, my television. Put plainly, I watch an extreme amount of television. Although my parents often tell me to turn off the television and do homework, I would watch television all day long if I could. To me, television is about more than just entertainment—it's about society, family, and communication. Television is not just an excuse to be lazy and become a couch potato; it is an artistic outlet and a method to express one's thoughts, feelings, and opinions.

When I was in fifth grade, my parents sat me down on my favorite couch and told me that they were getting a divorce because my dad is gay. Along with my shock and sadness toward the announcement, I felt awkward, judged, and confused because I did not truly comprehend the idea of homosexuality, nor was I comfortable telling my friends or even hearing my mother talk to relatives about our personal family business. As a child who never wanted to show weakness or emotion, I turned to television as a distraction, a way to escape my problems and ease the pain of what I perceived as a broken family. Television became my outlet, and along the way, I found *Gilmore Girls*, a show which taught me about life, love, and relationships. I connected with the main characters, Lorelai and Rory Gilmore, a mother and daughter who reminded me of the relationship between my mother and me. Lorelai was learning how to be a single parent and teach her daughter solid values just like my mother was doing. The close friendship between the two characters helped bring me closer to my mother and strengthened our relationship. Television and my spot on the couch healed my soul and allowed me to see that there is no such thing as a "normal" family. In my crazy, wonderful, perfect family, I learned that we accept everyone for who they are, even if society does not agree. Life has not been easy for my mother, father, and me, but we have also stayed united, even in the toughest moments of our lives.

My great-grandmother, who turned 100 in May, taught my mother that friendships can last even when marriages do not, a message that has become a staple in our households. Today, I can proudly state that my dad is gay without feeling ashamed or nervous because I love him regardless of the gender he is attracted to. My father has been happily married for almost a year and he is an amazing human being who I will love always and forever. My parents are the two strongest people and closest friends I have known and will ever know. Together, my mother, father, and stepfather have raised me to be the independent, mature, strong-willed, and well-rounded young woman that I am. My family is weird but also normal, and I will be forever grateful to have experienced such diversity in my childhood.

Television helped me see the true value of family. When I grow up, I want to pursue a career in television because it is important for people of all ages to understand the value of using the screen to tell a story and teach positive values. I want to bring joy to society and help others persevere in the face of challenging life changes.

NANA'S EULOGY

December 2, 2016

Frances Wallach Weissberger Schwartz
Zichrona l'vracha [May her memory forever be a blessing]
May 10, 1913 – December 2, 2016

Today I stand before you to eulogize my grandmother, Nana
Banana.
What a life!

I bring you radio station 103.5-FWWS. Frances Wallach
Weissberger Schwartz. We play Frank Sinatra all day, 24/7,
seven days a week.

After talking to Cantor Larry Eschler, my spiritual advisor,
yesterday, I consulted with Nana's big dictionary. You know the
one—it sits on a high pedestal handmade by my grandfather,
Poppop, in the TV room, near the blue chair.

To eulogize is to praise highly. I got this, Nana.

As Nana taught us all, "Love never divides; it multiplies."

It's really an easy story to follow. SO—keep up, people. Nana did.
And she passed her legacy to ALL of us in three families,
spanning four generations.

There's friendship. Marriage. Births. Death. Divorce. Another
marriage. Back to friendship.

When I was a kid, after a day spent at Jones Beach, playing putt-

putt and going to Nunley's Carousel and Amusement Park, Nana and I would sit outside on the patio, and she would draw my family tree. She taught me who is who. She never used the term "blood" relative, "stepson," or "half-brother." Never. We were family. There were no in-laws, outlaws or x-laws. I repeat, we are a family.

I always said to Nana, "Are you sure we aren't related?" She would look at me with that reassuring smile that only Nana had, place her hand over mine, and say, "Well, Becky, if you go far enough back, we are."

When Liz was in elementary school, she sat at that same patio table with Nana, and I watched while she passed the family-tree legacy to her great-granddaughter. A few days later, Liz looked at her father and me and explained:

"There's God
Then Nana.
Then Mommy and Daddy."

It's no secret in this room today that Nana and I have a special bond. After all, I am writing a book based on the things she has taught me. She guided me just like she has guided you—through many family crises.

Can you imagine how many secrets are resting in her house?

Keep talking. Be resourceful. Accept, adjust...life moves forward. Tomorrow is another day. Everything in moderation.

When my father, little Bobby, started Nana's birthday celebration on her 75th birthday, I started calling Nana by her age. 75. 76. 77. You get the gist. When people say to me, especially after we celebrated Nana's 100th birthday, "You have good genes," I simply smile as Nana would have and say, "Thank you."

What I respect and admire most about my Nana is her attitude. She took life and ALL its ups and downs and celebrations and she lived it—*with* YOU.

Last night I listened to Broadway tunes and Frank Sinatra to gather strength and reflect on this eulogy. Two things Nana loves—her Playbills and Frank. She listened to him every Sunday morning. She sure "did it my way."

To our beloved Nana, Mom, Aunt Frances. Although your physical presence is no longer with us, may we all carry you in our hearts and teach the legacy of a remarkable, inclusive family tree. *L'chaim* [to life].

THE BRIDGE TO HOPE & HEALING

TheBridgetoHopeandHealing.com

Explore products and services...

- ❖ Inspirational Keynotes
- ❖ Interactive Trainings
- ❖ Community Collaborations
- ❖ Building Bridges with Becky Podcasts

Connect with the author...

Becky S. Corbett, MSW, ACSW
Member of the Academy of Certified Social Workers
John Maxwell Team Certified Coach, Speaker, and Trainer

 @BeckySCorbett

 BeckySCorbett

 Info@BSCorbettConsulting.com

BSCorbett Consulting, LLC

BSCorbettConsulting.com

BSC supports you through your
organizational, professional,
and personal growth.

53879931R10061

Made in the USA
Columbia, SC
24 March 2019